JOSEPH

AND

THE VERY COLORFUL COAT

by Sunny Griffin

Illustrated by Donna Lee Hill

DID YOU KNOW...
Jacob had twelve sons, and Joseph was his favorite?

DID YOU KNOW... Joseph and his brothers helped their father by watching over his flock?

DID YOU KNOW...
Jacob gave Joseph a wonderful gift, and Joseph's brothers were jealous?

DID YOU KNOW...
Joseph's gift was a new, very colorful coat?

DID YOU KNOW...
One night, Joseph had a dream that made his brothers very angry when he told them about it?

DID YOU KNOW...
Jacob sent Joseph to the fields to check on his brothers and the sheep?

DID YOU KNOW... Joseph's brothers took away his very colorful coat and threw Joseph into a deep pit?

DID YOU KNOW... Merchants from another land bought Joseph from his brothers and sold him as a slave in faraway Egypt?

DID YOU KNOW...
Joseph's brothers lied
and told their father
that Joseph had been
killed by a wild animal?

DID YOU KNOW...
They tore Joseph's very colorful coat into pieces and gave it back to their father?

DID YOU KNOW...
Jacob was very sad and missed Joseph very much?

DID YOU KNOW...
Joseph became a great leader in Egypt, just as God had planned?

Years later, Joseph saw his family again, and he forgave his brothers.

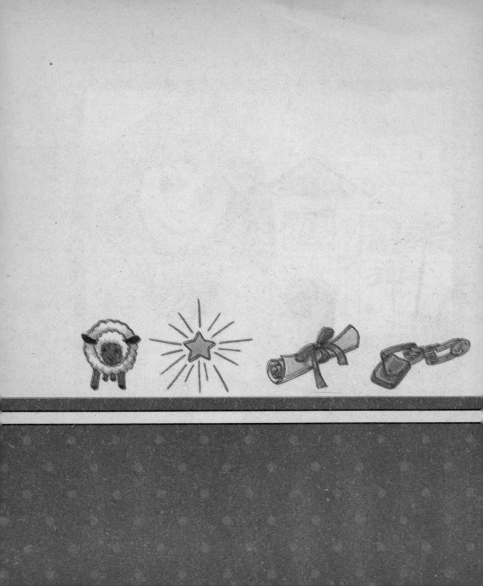